# Parallel Moons

*Evelyn Leigh*

# Parallel Moons

*Evelyn Leigh*

ISBN 13: 978-1-955338-09-7

Cover design & Illustrations by Kelly Gardner
Printed in the United States of America

## POCAHONTAS PRESS

DUBLIN, VA
POCAHONTASPRESS.COM

*For my friends, Tim Farris, Cheryl Van Balen, and Dusty Larrabee, all dying tragically by their own hand or another's. To my parents, who both served in WWII, and my husband whose love and companionship have sustained me. Many thanks to Kelly Gardner for her support and her amazing illustrations.*

*And, as always, to all of the kitties I have ever had who have given me purrs and comfort when I needed reminders that life and Nature are miracles in the present moment on our fragile planet.*

- E.L.

# Contents

# February's Dream

Thinned trees
Savagely stripped
Hold against winter's wind
Fearfully longing for warm light
Earth's hands.

# Suburban Basts

Felines-
Fixed in such a human state,
Ride on my shadow every moment.
Ears pricked at the sound of the
kitchen cabinet—bag rattle.
Pavloved out of a natural existence.

Two hissing beauties
Find bees and moths to stalk.
Gazing from my sliding window,
Glass hidden-
Eyes to the wooded slopes.

Striped and masked,
A great fielding camouflage is lost
In all this walled protection.
Rounded amber eyes
ready for a night prowl,
Grow dim and pale
In a full-mooned evening.

My yellow hand-made afghan
is the only soft comfort-
A reminder of young content.
They paw and paw this woolen animal
As if practicing for the freedom
of the first hunt.

They smile at me with eyes slit.
Roll over and beg for a belly rub.
With paws lifted and quivering meows,
These felines rest and wait for my every move,
Suckled to a wasteland of
Carpet and linoleum.

# Primordial Waste

Tap-wing in the trees,
Nightly flight in the boughs,
Touch this dingy, city apartment
With sensual wishes.

Wings fluttering, and chirping
Move and call me like sirens.
The street lights, so close,
Outline the bridge-
Lengthening onto a black, concrete skin.

Hard animals hissing
Across stubby aisles-
Searching the vanishing point,
Miles into the distance.

Winged and footed ancients lurking in
The reaching, rooted green,
Cry behind opaque shadows,
With whimpering surrender.

Deals of oppression

Cauterized the ligatures that balanced us once.

There is no going back

Or rising from the organic.

# SiddArthur

Buddha kitty,
Inspired by great Catness,
Rounds down to greet the floor
With an accepting of hands.
Respecting nose touches
And curious sniffs,
He stills the fearful others.

A fullness of being
Offered in soft purrs.
The meditative sound of the feline Om
Carries vibrations through all doubt,
Taming my heart---dissolving chaos
Into flowing simplicity.

# Snow

The silence of the falling snow
      has given voice to frozen rain,
Tapping my window with pecking bird sounds.

It wakens me to the warmth of the radiators.
I know I am swaddled and safe.

Veils shroud the cemetery
Next to my road, a peaceful stretch of lives-
Contrails for the rest of us.

Sometimes deer have their babies there and
I see the doe eye the fawns
As they prance between the markers.

Foot prints of children next door at play.
Moms carefully observing a legacy.

I lean back in simple being with impermanence
      as all covers my awareness
With the lightness of snow.

# Breath

The breath plows me like a great hand.
Sifts the jagged edges; smooths this landscape-
The effortless gardener.

An expansive blossoming, my heart billows,
Extends into the clouds with sweet wings-
Ripens a potential, untapped.

Then the emptying, dropping deep into a pause of
dark nurturing.
I follow the river of the heart,
Now flowing.

And in the wake of it, I release all attachment
Like a softening grip-
Merging endlessly into the lightness of space.

# Cat

I want to be embodied cat.
Rubbed by all, supplying soft hums.

Peaceful, radiant life-
Pads for feet.
Boundless energy
And never-ending sleep.

Smiles exposed, limbs running nowhere.
Soft paws hover skyward.

Mystic eyes penetrate,
Seeing forever through the obscure.
Throat sounds effervescent
And comforting.

Sounds spilling a divine elixir,
Expand into the universe.

# Surya Chandra Dance

The sun fires and establishes me
In a fixed stare, gazing through my
Gauzy scarf that shuts the sharpness out.
The heat is a comfort,
Penetrating savage as it hammers me in the chair.

Day now dissipating,
Light squeezed from an orange sky
Like a breath exhaled.
The moon begins to borrow illumination
But gradually gives its rounded fullness to
Crescent thinness—fading.

New moon opaque and
Faceless as it loses day.
Painted shadows brushing over
As opposites above, married like swans
For a moment—the pointed stars
Drizzle a dimmed sky.

Gradual darkening keeps all hidden

Without obligation or question.

Most wait eternities for eclipses like that.

This is what is left me

After a passing of two great extremes.

# Surfing

You, the wave,
Me, the shore.
We are carried
By the natural ride of it.
My eyes close and I see
Water and moons and translucent
Blues reflecting the shimmering dome.

Liquid swells pour over me in streams.
In silence
I rise and bloom,
Nurturing an oppressed desire.
I was once protected
By such destructions.

Leave me here
Where Luna rules
And restores simple light,
Flickering on this ocean of purity-
My heart at rest
In your embrace of waves.

# Wings

Luminous moth
Drawn to a dim garden light
on 9th Street-
Harsh realities
Scraping loud and unnoticed.
Fluttering, pale green and strange,
A translucent crucible,
Giving rise to a moment of strength
That appeals and speaks to me in its simplicity.
Isolation, ragefully manifesting,
Trapped in the diffused light-
Left behind by the lunar moth
Who abandoned all of us here,
On fire and wanting.

# The Trees

A quiet permission
Ignited an inner hue-
Loosened a caged need.
It leans into me here
At the trees where we met,
Long before their rooting.
The leafy, peeling birches
Stand aligned and circled
Around our vivid secrecy-
Bowing to the watery flow,
Seamlessly passing between us
Like clear rivers.

A crescent moon hangs
Weightlessly,
Perfecting these moments
And exposing our shared alchemy
Without hesitation.
So different from the night
I spent here alone
When there were no trees
Surrounding an idle heart-
With nothing

But the star-held sky's,
Mystical gaze-
When you were too clouded
To see me.
Only the distant spirals
Drawing me deep,
Pulling me in,
Veiling my roots,
Inviting release.

But now, our canopy of branches
Reach their signatures into
The waves whose gravity
Embraced me then.
A raw dancing here
In the summer thickness,
As we are stilled
Among the birches,
Breathing each other
With committed silence-
As if the trees planted us here
With a curious knowing.

# Night Unfolding

Visions kept from me
Like cats seeing at night.
I question any reason for feeling;
How it puzzles me that I feel
When there is a void of emotion.

I want to drop dead
Flat on my unseen face.
But last night the sky enfolded me
Into her distant waves,
Circling the moon in gentle worshiping streams.
Touching the opaque stillness,
I received the embrace.

Visions kept from me.
A dark and epileptic sky of lights
Offered a momentary respite from the unearthing of
bones.
Numbness claimed me
In this place of grief.

# Fierce

Look within
Beneath all facades-
Down into the secrets
Embedded in raw bone,
Until all cracks out of the marrow
Like trembling leaves
To be seen and touched.

Stand hard
In the cold sharp wind
Of transformation,
As it rises
Out of the heart's crevice-
Liquidating the
Ice of the un-said.

# Emptying

Discover me
Within my own awakening-
Inside something that turns for nothing.
The fluency of feeling
Alive in the mythical, spiraling dance.

The rain leaves a misty home,
Forcing black streets to mirror
A dark quiet,
Awareness shifts to a timeless flight.

Connection was lost somewhere
Between the chaos of your death
And a need for that
Calm abiding,
Where you are.

# Night Sparks

Dark brings quiet.
No mystery but stillness.
No madness, but the shadows playing.
The perfection of silence.
Blooms with the escape from day,
Spreads like morphine
After the prick of a needle.

Melting into the river of my coffin bed,
The ceiling begins to dance with exceptions-
Light flashes weave and flow.
Gazing at the ethereal
Creatures above, hovering-
Drawing close the sad ones
Into the velvety cloak.

# The Huntress

Where are you?
You who entered my house
And left with a gradual
Letting go.
I have been here for ages
Fighting your voice and
Return to you, half-embittered.
The house has changed,
Although untouched and dispirited-
Teased by your vague reflections.

Dead climbs around me
In this house of stone.
Your seed has taken refuge
In another time.
The wanderer-a white cloud
Seeking a life to shadow.

Where are you?
You who half-enters me now,
Testing me as if the effort futile,

Then, leaving with a sudden blow.

I see no remorse.

The indifference, pervasive.

In the mindless struggle,

Your capture will prove a win.

# Solitary Confinement

My bed,
The fuzzy warm lover,
Allows me electric arches and
Luxurious space.
Sheets quietly roam my corners
Like heavy feathers over
Thick, shrouded energy-
Whirling suppressed and mute.

It's easy here.
Open and thirsty.
Resistance weakens,
Melting rhythmic with
The cresting of this sharp edge.
A sun-beaten glacier
Breaking from within.

My hands,

Extensions of the boxy hammock,

Glide the cold exterior

In an attempt to replicate

Each primal stroke, now so intangible.

Little death building floods me

As an image of your eyes

Pours over me like violent waterfalls.


A sense of your form

Deepens into my elements,

Taking me from the dry embrace

Of this necessary furniture squared around me.

I stray so easily.

Touch from this perspective

Lingers, and holds no loss.

# Wind Chimes

Hearts lying in snow-frozen ponds.
Twigs from trees fall
  lightly down-
  disturbing the eruption.

Shadows whimper and ripple
As heat waves-
  moving upward-
  forming a mirage of ghosts.

Wind rages to loneliness
And a perennial
  hungering inward-
  touching stale senses.

Dreams unattainable
Intangible, like death
  unfolding and vanishing
  like water freezing.

# Mid-Day at Valley View

Alstroemeria blooms somewhere;
Probably a warm jungle
Where moss hangs moist
Like green rain.

The lady at the florist shop
Said they were like lilies.
But they jumped out at me
In their variegated form,
Like you, fourteen years ago,
Driving the Barracuda, wearing your hat,
To rescue me from this train within.

I ran through the mall at mid-day-
Deaf to noisy preparations for Christmas;
Blind to the stares and gestures of others;
Obsessed, like a shadow running
To join the opaque symmetry of you.

The numerous times I waited for calls,
Embroidering moments on linen.

Content at the hearing of your voice.

And now, lingering and cut,

Like this strange flower

That flickered for such a momentary reign.

# Noises

The breath, the breath
Comes echoing from the walls,
Down the deep aisles-
Reminds me of your presence
In a twisted life.

The bubbles rise and tinkle.
At least the fish are at ease,
Swimming in the sea dome.

Darkness surrounds
The noises of our home.
It cannot hear-
I will not hear.

# Lady Three

The White Goddess is your monolith.
Three-sided face in misty clouds
Keeps coming back to me
And into you
Forced illusion taking control.

Her beauty intrigues your inner maleness
As you reach out and touch the image,
Flinching at any thought of that power,
Holding back, putting the desire away,
To be put upon me at night under
Candle and leather.

Fantasy driven to lusty vengeance,
A moth in light singed on a moment.
The lady of love and hatred
Spreads her green vision in your eyes
Until you mold me to her weight.

Reality and ritual separated the
Great Rite performed on a J.C. Penney bed
At full moons and midsummer.

The trueness and realness of my womanhood
Forgotten in ideal celebrations.

Watching from the corner, the mother clearly stands
In my path, while you applaud introductions.
You've allowed the mother-induced protection
From another's hold—changing your will,
Examining the tone of this Wuthering bond.

A calm sets in, takes a new place at the table.
Changes constant, unnoticed, unfelt.
The Destroyer stands stone at bed-foot
While I lie blindfolded and strapped
To your thoughts of her in me.

A helpless pawn cornered in misunderstanding.
I will become a Lady of Three
For the bald, horned man.
As I step into this dark water,
I feel a sad love begin to twist and fold.

# Crossroads

We walked across the parking lot-
    black ocean ticked in lamp light.
The stranded grocery cart you kicked
    released frustration for metal and man.

It wasn't in that darkness that I found you.
    Only years later, when oneness fell,
did I see your face, your real face, in the
    faces splitting me from you.

I cried child; bent pain in deep waters,
    let distance seep in, no longer able to see.
Feelings came in rushes;
    paranoid jolts of loss and leaving.

Your roots deep and sturdy.
    My joining with you left
A latent impression
    grayed in your wake.

# Night Terror

Darkness
Hands reaching toward me
Disappearing as I turn.
A door is opened
Movement is my judgment.

Light
Her shadow lies beneath the table
And in her stillness
I find my confusion.
The other stands in a barren,
Motionless facade
Waiting for me to break.

Rage
Wraps around me
As I stare into her face
The glance did it--
Ice eyes
On a background of vengeance.

Body
Grieving and convulsing
Confessing all.
I wake
To my own howling.

# Hands

Mom's fingers were like feathers.
They were always old though, thin and wrinkly.
She wore her rings carefully and sparkled-
   A strange past coupled aside work and family-
   She stands at the kitchen sink waiting for the
   Next round of cutting knives.

She really hated the childhood rowdiness
The constant talking, crying, fighting-
Always finding some way to soothe and
   Lull us into sleep;
   Just a quiet respite of images,
   Floating on clouds.

Then, Daddy's hands- rugged stubby fingers
Gripping mechanical pencils;
Penciling maps, words, electrical grids on linen.
   Ideas in straight lines and calculations-
   Weathered and calloused
   From war and repetitive duties.

Even then mine were veined stubbiness-
Every instrument beyond my attainment,
Thick with aging blue spiders.
   Impoverished notes from a wasted piano-
   A dissonant offering, but welcomed
   Through the shared flat gaze

# Third Stage

It's like Jimmy's fate.
Raging in the streets
Losing it gradually
Like the waning moon-
Howling comes later.

First, the stares.
Only to avert the eyes.
It all boils over
In a volcanic, freakish event.
Heads turn away
From the grotesque, it's instinctive.

The tears well, but dam up.
Verbiage consumes me.
Clues, always clues-
Brushed off with a
Quick flick of a finger.

Here it is, again and again,
Jimmy's demise.

The black canopy
Sliding down, claiming the light.
Onlookers, shaking it off.
Silence yells indignation.

# The Rise and Fall

The high rise bed held you
many nights.
Punished,
Reading it over and over
As a fanatical preacher
sweating sin and greed.
Hoping for a reason.
It didn't come.
Only pages yellowing-
A binding cracking the Reich.

Maybe you were a lost Jew
Waiting to suck in the gas.
Those nights never paid.
Nazis in the south
with mouth gold.
Watches from Italy
stealing time.
Darkness on the high-rise
left you with flashbacks.
The Rise and Fall
on the radiator
never burned.

# The Purpose of Cans

I used to be full of soup.
Just Campbell's, nothing exotic.
Fed the girls lunch or supper.
Then they flew outside like
Dragonflies searching a bush.

When they left me, their mom
Rinsed me out---trashed me.
But the girls would run back
To dig me out-
Save me from
the inevitable existence as
refuse.

God, I wish I had hidden
under the paper towel in the plastic can.
Instead, my destiny revealed under the tree
when David put his foot on me,
started to count.

Everyone would run.
I was so confused at first.

I couldn't see them from the
sidewalk, though I could hear them
conspiring against me.

In July's muggy heat
I felt the earth thunder
Underneath me, created
by their sprints.
The first dent kicked into my side.

Perhaps this was fun; this game at my expense.
It was beyond my comprehension.
I had to let go, surrender to my fate.
After all, I was outside in the thick of the sun,
warmed by the brief freedom of adolescence.

Becoming an observer and
Victim at the same time, wondering-
Is this what it means to be a sentient being?
Imbued with a discovery that
It must be the anticipation of pain that hurts.

# Ode to Dylan

Do not go gentle?
Laughable!
I can question that reality.
Invite the veil with heavy surrender
And energetic resolve.
Alone at the inevitable summit,
Witnessing embodied dissolution.
My spirit-self in osmosis,
Merging with the universal stream
Like the trail of a comet, bright-
Letting go of the darkness
That pounds me like heartbeats,
Into this good night.

# Cancer Rising

The girly magazine at the doctor's office
Said Cancer was rising.
Metamorphosis mis-shaping me
Like a great explosion-
The Big Bang gone internal.

It could be the death of me-
A simple coming and going.
Who am I to doubt its presence?
This life form manifested in
A busy cellular display
Demanding strict attention.

I want to wear it as a gift
From the constellation re-birthing me.
These sassy red giants expanding into me
With dirty fingers,
Offering a half-form,
Flat and unresponsive.

Somehow it all slips off of me.
Melts with cold explanations
Of scars, poison, tattoos.
You still see me through a
Thick mannequin skin-
A blackened rite of passage.
I am born in this ash.

# Friday Night

Kevin in dreadlocks
Emitting color on a Friday night.
The room filled with disillusioned teenagers
And a wannabe beat poet.

Another writes an ode to her rug.
Giving it center stage and
A significant existence,
Detailed with passion and rug ego.

The undoubtable conclusion exposed.
The young knowing death is old,
Ready to snuff out newness
And slow to rise
To a calling.

# Castle Van Balen

I remember you in yellow
On a crisp beach evening.
A blonde in blonde-
Smooth pearl skin covering deep pools.

A goddess-like flow
Walking through sleazy honky-tonk,
Gave fluency to tacky shell-jewelry
And empty come-ons.

Your dance conjured needs.
Spliced hope upon waves and stone.
A blonde in blonde,
Drawn into false security-

Absorbed inside the chemical rush
Of space and blankness.
A territory of pearls marked
Like dust on gossamer silk.

Forced into non-being.
Violence weighted the heaviness
Masking a soft gaze into the light.
Reality split the quiet moments
For the blonde in blonde.

# Prophecy

(Fashioned after: "The River Merchant's Wife: A Letter" by
Ezra Pound)


While my hair was long on my shoulders
I sat on a hill, fantasizing.
You walked toward me, making faces.
You nestled next to me, sketching silliness.
And we went on studying-
Two connected people, headed in
Different directions.

At 26, I married a friend.
I laughed.  I remembered you often.
Curling up sleepily, I visited you.
Called to you a thousand times.
I looked back.

Ladies electric, easily within your reach.
Your eyes shined through them,
Too intense for me for so long.
I turned into my inadequacy.

At 42, I went wild.
I desired everything to merge.
Always, always, always-
Why should I settle for less?

But while my hair was gone,
I fell in the summer heat-
Saw beaches and sailboats
On the Mediterranean horizon-
They healed me.

I grew brighter
Because you sat near me
In the darkness,
Offering your lightness;
Seeing me older,
Thinking me young.

# Venus on the Half-Shell

After the biting sting of tears,
Sadness permeates
Like a quick, seeping wound.
A laden cloak that wears me,
Rain-flooded and uncomfortable.

The visits transport and lift me
From the wintery heaviness,
Quietly filling me
With whispered violets-
Blooming their petals, erotic.

Your hands ride me, torturous
And light in their attention,
Resonating a liquid, harmonic chord.
Cool, watery pools emerge episodically
Between glances.

Salty vessel reaching upward.
Sensations climbing like a slow
Provocative dance.-
Compelling and karmic.

Your presence protects me
Like a great shell
Holding a black pearl
In a turbulent sea,
Rocking.

There is a rippling
Through the night
While I rest
In the buoyancy.

# Skin

Skin, covers the soul but
Not the heart,
Bleeding empty-
A vast cave, un-fillable.
Seamless and child-stricken
Sipping a creamy latte.
Who could have asked for more?
Until it melted on the floor
Exposing wounds.
Sometimes white, sometimes dark-
Giraffe spotted and confusing.

Skin cuts easily;
Invites scars to tell a story.
Imperfections becoming more
Imperfections- morph ghost-like
Onto the scene.
A numbness comes when stroked,
Lying down fixes it.
Gravity smoothes it back to flat, youthful silkiness-
A sleight of hand.

Skin, disguises intention but
Not action
Chevroned for the fight.
The shade of it determines a fate,
Casts the dice for worthiness-
Opaque coverings offer no shield from night sticks or
knees.
Shoving it into a smothering dirt
Postpones the inevitable
Pushing down of the alabaster marble statues
That hover and boot the lies.

Skin, thick and thin-
Obscures the unerring spirit-
Bunches up like a crumpled receipt.
Exposing the slow unfolding of time-
A gnawing bone thrown to the wolves
As a final gift to the ravenous ground.
The ethereal arises; dissolves
As consciousness curls inward toward
That final dance.

# Cold

Winter arrived early.
The leaves never changed.
Reds and yellows lost
To the summer greens-
Hanging, black and withered.
The emptiness washed over me the night before
Like a familiar waterfall--strange and hard.

The gown shrouds me again.
Forced to wear it , I am back
To where it started-
Alone in the thicket.
A vacant sky casting long, jagged shadows
Through my eyes-
empty and robotic.

The trees, voiceless and crumbling,
Barely see me.
Even in the moonlight, the dark takes you.
Cold, cold winter laid you down,
Lays me down hollow and surrendering.
All is still and silent.
I see you.

# Miscarriage

Caught in the rush of severe heat,
A desperate gripping that mimics
The touch of dry ice.
Smooth addiction consuming me,
Driven by erotic eyes.

Gazing in stillness,
Images sparking
Lava in my roots.
A sponge wet and heavy,
Waiting.

I sit with this burning,
Inhibited and jailed,
Drawn to you by centrifugal force,
Averting your reflection
Out of fearful necessity.

It's a pattern-

Formless but predictable.

Nothing is allowed from the heart.

The welling of the unexpressed expands

Full and stillborn,

Drawing back into me for containment.

# Parallel Moons

Moon-struck silver,
Pointed sharp and curious,
Astounds my heart and
Wells a distant memory-
A cicada in the reaching dark.
I am incomplete and have
Emerged and surfaced
Glimpsing a small opening.

A whisper crossed over me
And settled here.
Spirited and soft
She is clear and pure,
Full-mooned and pregnant with grace.
I hesitate at such touches
Then embrace them,
Woman absorbed.

Riding on this crescent
I am torn upon bright acuities.
Rising wide and shrouded
He is absent and descending,
New mooned and dark
With rejection.
I remain faithfully,
Hidden by conflicting light.

# Dark Acoustic

A craving for echoing sounds builds
Within the walls of a dimly lit bar.
Crowded but empty. Voices inarticulate
    from clinking ice cubes and laughs.
A few jokes and flirts between sips.

In here I feel heat, light from the instruments.
Gritty hands slide down
The fret length, gripping taut strings-
    the bridge stroking the wooden throat.
And tones of calloused fingers, extra.

Would you hold me that way?
Treat me hard with chords and weightless
Mellow rifts, bound and
    wedded, hypnotize with energy
Directed into the bone of an electric grief.

# Catatonic Mirage

No longer a physical presence.
Death pierced it. It was summer and humid.
Remembering is all I have to keep me alive.
Like the wild call I hear from the sky dome,
Or any strings that hold my eyes-
Pulling me away from the solid earth,
I find refuge in staring through air.
The sun finds a way over me.
Deep sand warms my toes
As space conjures me into
A still point that waits beyond my reach.
My grave there red in the night,
All here is forgotten
And the light calls like the driftwood
of a sea home.
Fluent as a bird on water,
floating away
Like the graces of timeless wings.

# Goddess Rebirth

Gaia's crinoline drapes our Earth.
Spying an observation
Over Her bas-relief surface,
Now scattered with crumbled bricks and suffocating
asphalt.
Lavender phlox straining through the cracks;
Flora and fauna buried daily in her sight.
Birth power of the feminine used for destruction,
     sinking into the blood-soaked Earth.

The night sky remains intoxicating,
Brisk and clear, gifting
Her belly with a future of
Green and blue-belled meadows.
Moving forests house resting eyes-
Leading us to a clarity of reflecting pools
And wishing wells,
     air of velvet pervades.

Day returns, all smiles and devil-consumed-
Exposes the plunder of neglect.
Guns cocked and aimed,
Ready for the shot.

Empowered by time
As Earth's fullness lies in stasis-
Protected at the hem of Her robe.
With all exposed, Gaia turns Her back,
Walks to a shaded grove where
Trees guard Her like armies and
She quietly waits Her own
    birthing of the sacred Moon.

# Silences

Within the circle of poets and artists
Exists a shared loneliness.
Your eyes conveyed it so quietly-
The blue that pierced me
With the soul of an ocean.
I couldn't speak.
I couldn't move.

I loved you from a place understood only
From the perspective of your death-
Never giving my love credit,
Thinking it embryonic
And girlish like giggles.
You sensed it.
You touched it.

If I had only rested my head on your heart,
I may have held you longer
Through intense summers lingering in heat;
Memories dotted as impressionistic forms.
Perhaps I will find you in the warm

Energy realm of spirits
Where your intimate blues
Open the silence and,
In that spaciousness,
We can speak.

# Acknowledgements

"Cancer Rising", Artemis Journal, 2019.

"The Trees", The Dauntless Raven/Virginia Western Community College, 2015.

"The Rise and Fall", Poetry Society of Virginia Anthology, 2003.

"Wind Chimes", Poetry Society of Virginia Anthology, 2003.

"Lady Three", Poetry Society of Virginia Anthology, 1993.

## About the Author

Evelyn Leigh, a life-long resident of Roanoke, Virginia, graduated from Radford College and Virginia Tech. She worked as a public mental health therapist for 25 years and currently teaches yoga classes locally, sometimes becoming inspired to write down little musings. Some poems have been published under variations of her full name, Evelyn Leigh Hicks Urquhart. Evelyn still lives in her native Roanoke, in the Grandin Village area, where she grew up and where she will always feel her roots.

About the Artist

Kelly Gardner, from Lynchburg, Va., has been a graphic designer for over 30 years. She lives a creative life in a small house with two fabulous, fat cats and a plethora of art supplies. She has a passion for sculpting creatures based on folklore and doing small illustrations and drawings.